The Colony of New Jersey

Susan Whitehurst

The Rosen Publishing Group's

PowerKids Press™

New York

For Great Aunt Dotty

Published in 2000 by The Rosen Publishing Group, Inc.
29 East 21st Street, New York, NY 10010

Copyright © 2000 by The Rosen Publishing Group, Inc.

Photo Credits: Cover and title page, pp. 1,11,15 © Super Stock; pp. 12 © Stock Montage; p. 4, 7, 8, 16, 20 © Granger Collection; p. 22 © FPG International; p. 19 © Bridgeman Art Library; p. 7 © North Wind Pictures; p. 22 Courtesy of Morristown/Morris Township Library;

First Edition

Book Design: Andrea Levy

Whitehurst, Susan.
    The Colony of New Jersey / by Susan Whitehurst.
        p.   cm. — (The library of the thirteen colonies and the Lost Colony)
    Includes index.
    Summary: Relates the history of the colony of New Jersey from its founding in 1664 to statehood in 1787.
    ISBN 0-8239-5480-3 (lib. bdg.)
    1. New Jersey—History—Colonial period, ca. 1600-1775 Juvenile literature. 2. New Jersey—History—1775-1865 Juvenile literature. [1. New Jersey—History—Colonial period, ca. 1600–1775. 2. New Jersey—History—1775-1865.]   I. Title. II. Series.
F137.W66 1999
974.9'02—dc21   99-14960
                                                                                                                    CIP

Manufactured in the United States of America

Contents

Settling the Land

For hundreds of years, the land that would later become New Jersey belonged to many Native American tribes. Beginning in the 1600s, people from Europe started coming to this area to settle in **colonies**.

In 1609, the **explorer** Henry Hudson came to America looking for a river that connected the Atlantic and Pacific Oceans. He hoped that this would be a quick way to get from Europe to Asia to buy silks and spices. There was no river like this, but since Hudson worked for a Dutch company in the Netherlands, the Dutch claimed all the land he explored and named it "New Netherlands."

◀ *Henry Hudson explores the coast of America.*

A Dutch Colony

In 1624, the Dutch built Fort Nassau on the Delaware River. Then in 1643, the Swedes (people from Sweden) came over and built Fort Elfsborg close to Fort Nassau. Both the Dutch and the Swedes wanted colonies in this area so they could buy furs from the nearby Iroquois Indians and sell them in Europe. The Dutch had claimed the land first, and wanted the Swedes to leave. In 1655, Peter Stuyvesant, the Dutch **governor** of New Netherlands, marched to Fort Elfsborg with a group of soldiers. He ordered the Swedes to give up the fort, and they surrendered without a fight.

Peter Stuyvesant's nickname was "Peg Leg Pete" because he had lost a leg and replaced it with a peg.

Peter Stuyvesant orders the Swedes to give up Fort Elsborg (against a map showing Fort Nassau and Fort Elfsborg). ▶

(EN)

BOUNDARY OF NE

Hwiskakimensi or
ed.Clay) Creek

Fort

kpeckans Sippunck
Minquas, Tasswairres. Elbe
nonck, Sandhoeck, Dutch Fort Casimir
or Christinah Cr Koffg
or Hvitlers (White
Creek

(Christeen)
Fort Trefaldighet 1651-1655 (NewCastle)

Strandwik
Strandviken

DELAWARE
SOUTH OR NEW

Obissquasoit

Asamo Hackingh
or
Varkens (Salem)
Creek

Oitsessingh

(SALEM)
English Colony from New Haven
1641+
Fort Nya Elfsborg 1643-1651 (Elsinborough Point)
Korten Revier (Alloways Creek)

ndrakung or Vattung
(Mill or Cob

chuylkill River)

on Creek)

nipack) C

ckan

Creek

BURLINGTON

Trinnekonck Island
Assatungh
Wiranth
(Assiscu

PHILADELPHIA

Dutch Fort Beversreede Kd

(Tacony)

Marachonjicla

Mölndal 1645
Nya Wasa 1645-
38
Nya Korsholm 1647-1653
Printz Hof
chnakonck
Tinicum

Wickquacoingh
Passajungh

Kackamensi

Nittabakonck

Pessenawanni

(Rancocas) C

(CAMDEN)

Rancoques

Poenpissingh

Struts

(Pensauken) Creek

Hjorte (Cooper's) Creek
Sassaëkon
Little Timber Creek

Sinsessingh

Rode Udden
(Red Bank)

Tetamekonck
(Big Timber)
Timmer

Dutch Fort Nassau 1623-1651

Tekoke

Mantes (Mantua) Creek
Kanokanick

NORTHERN BOUNDARY OF NEW SWEDEN BY PURCHASE FROM INDIANS BY PRINT

Memirako

Hackomene Hackingh

Arwames

UTHERN BOUNDARY OF NEW SWEDEN BY PURCHASE FROM INDIANS BY HOLLENDER, 1641.
RECOGNISED IN INSTRUCTIONS TO PRINTZ, 1642.

Swedesborough)

or Aldermans

(Oldmans) Creek

Narraticon (Raccoon) Creek

Assueticon
or Riddare

NEW

JERSEY

(D

Creek)

(BRIDGETON)

MED GUDS NADE SVERIGES GÖTES OCH

England Takes Over

By the 1660s, England already had colonies in America, but King Charles II wanted another. He gave New Netherlands to his brother James, the duke of York. There was just one problem. New Netherlands belonged to the Dutch. James would have to take it from them. James was the head of the English navy. In May 1664, he sent warships to New Netherlands. Governor Stuyvesant had fewer men and weapons than the English and surrendered without a fight. The large area that was New Netherlands became an English colony and was renamed New York, in James's honor.

New York was named after James, the duke of York, who later became King James II.

New Jersey

In 1664, James gave part of New York to two friends, Sir George Carteret and Lord John Berkeley. Sir Carteret came from the Isle of Jersey in England, so James named the new colony New Jersey. Sir Carteret and Lord Berkeley were the **proprietors**. They charged rent to settlers who moved onto their land.

To get English colonists to move to New Jersey, the proprietors offered cheap land and freedom of religion. Many settlers came to New Jersey, but Sir Carteret and Lord Berkeley were not very good leaders. In 1672, the Dutch reclaimed New Jersey, and the proprietors weren't able to get it back until 1674.

Many settlers came to New Jersey in search of religious freedom. ▶

Gens

ROQVO-

IS

kensivm]

YORK

Massachu-

setts   Col

C. Ann

Gloucester
Manchester
Marble Head

Onoida

New

Albanie

N. Hampton

Springfield

Boston Town

Lyn

Mohocks Castle

Anne
Schenecta
Albany
Fort

New

Deerfield

Hadley

Squab

Hartford

Wethersfield

Weymouth
Cohasset Roc

Scituate

Marsfield

York

Connecti

Middle
town

Plimouth

C. Co

Barn
stable

cot Col

Col

Hudson

OCEANUS

New Tom
Sandy Point
Shrowsbury
Shark R.
Manasquam R.
Barnegat
Bay
Joe Sandy Land
Little Egg Harbour
Great Egg Harbour
New Inlet

Long Isl.

New York
Ulrichs Plein
Salisbury Plein

Newtown

Block I.

Martha's
Vinyard

Nantucket

New
Crow

Nant

Scho

Montang Pt
Gardeners I.
Elizabeth I.

East Hampton
Feversham
S. Hampton

Bergen Cou

NEW JERSEY

JERSEY

Essex C

N. Barbados

Perquenuck

Delaware

N. Branch

Falls

WEST

Burlington

EAST

Moumouth
Cou

Bucks C

Philadel
phia Co

Philadelphia

Salham

Germantown

Chester
chichester

Brandy

Newcastle

C. May
Cou

Woodland

Mour C.
York Col

C. May

Baltimore I.

PENSILVANIA

LAND

New Jersey Divides

In 1674, Lord Berkeley sold his part of New Jersey to two **Quakers**. The Quakers were a religious group that was **persecuted** in England, and many Quakers wanted to move to America. New Jersey was divided into East and West Jersey, and the Quakers moved into West Jersey. Then Sir Carteret's widow decided to sell East Jersey. She sold it to 24 English, Irish, and Scottish men, most of whom were Quakers. Neither East nor West Jersey were very successful. In 1702, they joined together and became a royal colony ruled by the king of England.

Quakers was a nickname given to members of the Religious Society of Friends, because their leader, George Fox, said they should "quake" or tremble before the Lord.

This map shows the division of New Jersey into East and West Jersey.

Life in the Colony

New Jersey was growing fast. By 1760, New Jersey had 60 towns and 94,000 colonists. Almost everybody farmed. They grew wheat, corn, and oats. They also raised cows, chickens, pigs, and sheep. Towns were usually made up of little more than a church, a courthouse, an inn, a general store, and a blacksmith's shop. Every town with 50 families or more had to have a school. The colony also had a college, the College of New Jersey, that began in 1747 with one professor and six students. Colonists on the sea coast made a living by fishing, whaling, and building ships.

> The College of New Jersey was moved to Princeton, NJ, in 1756 and renamed Princeton. Today it is one of the best colleges in the country.

Many colonists raised cows and sheep. ▶

New Jersey Joins the Fight Against England

When England won the last French and Indian War in 1763, it owed a lot of money for soldiers, weapons, and forts. To make money, England decided to **tax** the colonies. Many colonists became angry and refused to pay the taxes, but people in New Jersey were not that upset at first. They liked their English governor, William Franklin, and business and farming in the colony were good. Then, in 1773, colonists in Boston threw 350 chests of English tea into the bay to protest the tax on tea. New Jersey decided to join the other colonies in the fight against England. A year later Greenwich, New Jersey had its own tea party, burning English tea in the village square.

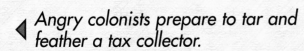

Angry colonists prepare to tar and feather a tax collector.

17

Getting Ready for War

The colonists were angry about how England was treating them. The colonists had to decide between staying British colonies or making a new nation. Colonists went to a meeting in Philadelphia in 1774, called the First Continental Congress. The colonists decided to ask King George III for fairer treatment of the colonies, but knew that they might have to go to war if he refused. New Jersey colonists wrote a state **constitution** that made new laws for the colony. New Jersey colonists were still not positive that they wanted to separate from England, though. They included a section in their constitution that said they would follow England's laws if the problems between the countries were settled.

Here is the historic building where the First Continental Congress met. ▶

New Jersey at War

The **Revolutionary War** began on April 19, 1775. Five New Jersey men traveled to Philadelphia to the Second Continental Congress. There they signed the **Declaration of Independence** on July 4, 1776. America's navy only had 50 ships, but hundreds of privately owned ships from New Jersey fought in the war. Nearly 100 Revolutionary War battles were fought in New Jersey. One of New Jersey's most famous soldiers was "Molly Pitcher." Molly followed her husband into battle to serve tired soldiers water from a pitcher. When her husband was injured, Molly took his place and fired his cannon. George Washington personally thanked Molly for her work. The Revolutionary War ended when the British surrendered to George Washington in 1781.

◀ *Molly Pitcher made New Jersey proud with her efforts in the war.*

New Jersey Becomes a State

To form a new government, representatives from all the states traveled to Philadelphia to write the Constitution. On December 18, 1787, New Jersey approved the Constitution and became the third state. New Jersey earned the nickname "**Cockpit** of the Revolution" because so many battles were fought there. Revolutionary War statues, like the one of George Washington above, stand in New Jersey today as reminders of its heroic Colonial past.

1609		1664		1787
Henry Hudson sails up the Hudson River and claims New Jersey for the Netherlands.	Swedish settlers arrive in New Jersey.	The English take control of New Jersey.	New Jersey signs the Declaration of Independence.	New Jersey adopts the Constitution and becomes the third state.
	1638		1776	

Glossary

cockpit (KAHK-pit) A place known for violent fighting.

colonies (KAH-luh-nee) A group of people who leave their own country and settle in another land, but who still remain under the rule of their old country's laws and leaders.

constitution (KAHN-stih-TOO-shun) A paper that explains how the government of a country or state will work.

Declaration of Independence (deh-kluh-RAY-shun UV in-duh-PEN-dints) A paper signed on July 4, 1776, declaring that the American colonies were independent of England.

explorer (ik-SPLOR-ur) A person who travels to different places to learn more about them.

governor (GUH-vuh-nur) An official that is put in charge of a colony by a king or queen.

persecuted (PUR-sih-kyoo-tid) When someone is attacked or treated badly because of his or her beliefs.

proprietors (pruh-PRY-uh-turz) People who were given a colony and could make laws for that colony and give or sell the land to others.

Quakers (KWAY-kurz) People who belong to a religion that believes in equality for all people, strong families and communities, and peace.

Revolutionary War (REH-vuh-LOO-shuh-nayr-ee WOR) The war that American colonists fought from 1775 to 1783 to win independence from England.

tax (TAKS) When the government makes people give money to help pay for public services.

Index

Web Sites:

You can learn more about Colonial New Jersey on the Internet:
http://people.csnet.net/~dpost/welcome.html